DID DEEPSEEK REALLY STEAL FROM OPENAI?

Truth and the New Battle for AI Dominance

The Secret War Behind the Future of Intelligence

Jackson Z. Scott

Table of Contents

Introduction

The world has entered a new era, one where intelligence is no longer bound to the human mind. Artificial intelligence, once a distant vision confined to the pages of science fiction, has become a powerful force shaping economies, industries, and the very fabric of society. At the center of this transformation is OpenAI, a company that, in just a few years, went from an ambitious research lab to an industry titan. Its models, particularly the revolutionary GPT-4, have redefined what machines can do—reasoning, writing, problem-solving, even simulating creativity in ways once thought impossible.

But no empire remains unchallenged forever. As OpenAI stood at the forefront of AI supremacy, a sudden and unexpected rival emerged from China—DeepSeek. A name virtually unheard of in the West, this startup burst onto the global scene with a model that seemed too powerful, too refined, and too competitive for a company of its size and resources. Almost overnight, DeepSeek R1 soared past ChatGPT to become the most downloaded AI assistant in the U.S. and across dozens of countries. It wasn't just another chatbot—it was an alternative, a competitor that, by some accounts, performed just as well, if not better, than OpenAI's best offerings.

That alone was enough to raise eyebrows. But then came the allegations. Reports surfaced that DeepSeek may have gained an unfair advantage—not through innovation, but through intellectual theft. According to sources within Microsoft, suspicious activity had been detected within OpenAI's systems, leading to an investigation into whether DeepSeek had extracted valuable data from OpenAI's API. If the accusations were true, this wasn't just a case of a startup outperforming an established giant—it was a case of a company possibly reverse-engineering OpenAI's breakthroughs by siphoning its knowledge, an act that could shake the foundations of the entire AI industry.

The implications were massive. This wasn't just about two companies fighting for dominance—it was about geopolitics, economics, and the future of global technological power. For years, the United States had maintained a lead in AI research, thanks to its access to cutting-edge chips, massive funding, and an unparalleled concentration of talent. But China, despite U.S. sanctions and restrictions on advanced semiconductors, had been quietly building its own AI ecosystem, determined to catch up—and perhaps even surpass—the West.

DeepSeek's rapid rise triggered a storm of speculation. Was this a David vs. Goliath moment, where a lean and efficient newcomer outmaneuvered the AI giants? Or was it a case of intellectual property theft, with DeepSeek simply repackaging OpenAI's advancements under its own name? The answer had the potential to reshape AI regulations, influence global policies, and shift the balance of technological power.

At stake is not just the reputation of a few companies but the very future of AI itself. If OpenAI's work could be replicated for a fraction of the cost, what would that mean for the billion-dollar AI race? If China could develop competitive models despite chip bans and Western restrictions, would the U.S. lose its edge in the most transformative technology of the 21st century? And if DeepSeek really did steal OpenAI's tech—how did they do it?

This book unravels the mystery behind one of the most controversial battles in modern AI history. It examines the players, the claims, the political undertones, and the economic consequences of a world where artificial intelligence is no longer just about innovation—but about control.

The war for AI dominance has begun. And in this war, knowledge isn't just power—it's everything.

Chapter 1: The Rise of OpenAI and the AI Gold Rush

In the early days of artificial intelligence, the concept of machines possessing human-like reasoning and problem-solving abilities was a distant dream. Scientists and engineers had long theorized about the possibility of artificial general intelligence—machines capable of understanding, learning, and adapting across a wide range of tasks just as a human would. But for decades, AI remained confined to narrow applications, excelling only in specific, predefined tasks like playing chess or recognizing patterns in images. That all changed with the emergence of OpenAI.

Founded in 2015 by a group of influential tech entrepreneurs, including Elon Musk and Sam Altman, OpenAI set out with a bold mission: to ensure that artificial intelligence benefits all of humanity. Unlike traditional AI companies that pursued profit-driven motives, OpenAI positioned itself as an independent research organization, committed to developing safe and ethical AI that would not be controlled by a single entity. Its vision was ambitious—pushing beyond specialized AI systems and working toward artificial general intelligence, a type of AI that could think, reason, and solve complex problems across different domains without needing explicit programming.

At first, OpenAI's progress was steady but incremental. The organization published groundbreaking research papers, built small-scale AI models, and contributed to the academic community. But everything changed when it introduced its Generative Pre-trained Transformer models—the GPT series. The launch of GPT-2 in 2019 was an eye-opener, demonstrating that AI could generate human-like text with remarkable fluency. This model could write essays, summarize articles, and even engage in open-ended conversations, raising both excitement and concerns about AI's potential.

But it was GPT-3, released in 2020, that truly transformed the field. With 175 billion parameters, GPT-3 was a colossal leap forward, capable of writing with an uncanny level of coherence and creativity. It could generate poetry, compose music lyrics, draft legal documents, and even mimic different writing styles with impressive accuracy. Suddenly, AI wasn't just a tool for automation—it was a creator, a conversationalist, and a potential replacement for countless knowledge-based jobs.

The impact of OpenAI's models extended far beyond research circles. GPT-3 became the foundation for a wave of AI-powered applications, from virtual assistants to content generators. Companies around the world integrated OpenAI's technology into their services, ushering in a new era of human-AI collaboration. The explosion of interest in large language models prompted OpenAI to transition from a non-profit research lab to a more structured corporate entity, partnering with Microsoft in a multi-billion-dollar deal that provided the computing power necessary to push AI capabilities even further.

The evolution continued with GPT-4, a model that set new benchmarks for reasoning, accuracy, and contextual understanding. Unlike its predecessors, GPT-4 demonstrated improved problem-solving skills, better fact-checking abilities, and a higher level of creativity. Businesses, developers, and researchers eagerly adopted the technology, integrating it into everything from education and healthcare to legal analysis and financial forecasting.

Yet, with success came scrutiny. As OpenAI's models became more powerful, concerns about misinformation, bias, and AI-generated deception grew. Governments and policymakers debated how to regulate these systems, fearing that uncontrolled AI development could lead to unintended consequences. Meanwhile, competitors scrambled to match OpenAI's breakthroughs, investing billions into their own AI research in an effort to build something even more advanced.

As OpenAI cemented its position as the leader in artificial intelligence, the rest of the world took notice. Rivals emerged, each seeking to challenge OpenAI's dominance in the space. But no one expected that a little-known startup from China would soon arrive on the scene with a model that appeared to rival OpenAI's best work. The AI race was about to take an unexpected turn, and OpenAI would soon find itself in the middle of one of the most controversial battles in modern technology.

As OpenAI's ambitions grew, so did the scale of its challenges. Developing cutting-edge artificial intelligence required immense computational power, vast datasets, and continuous research—a trifecta that demanded resources far beyond what a single research organization could sustain on its own. By the time OpenAI had unveiled GPT-3, it was clear that to push AI to the next frontier, it needed a partner with deep pockets, state-of-the-art infrastructure, and the willingness to bet big on the future of intelligence. That partner turned out to be Microsoft.

The relationship between OpenAI and Microsoft started as a strategic collaboration, but it quickly evolved into something far more significant. In 2019, Microsoft invested $1 billion into OpenAI, securing an exclusive partnership that would give the tech giant access to OpenAI's groundbreaking models while providing OpenAI with the massive computational resources it needed to train even more advanced systems. This investment wasn't just about funding—it was about control, influence, and the strategic positioning of AI within Microsoft's vast ecosystem.

At the heart of this partnership was Microsoft's Azure cloud computing platform. AI models like GPT-3 and GPT-4 required immense amounts of processing power to function effectively, and training these models from scratch demanded specialized hardware that only a handful of companies in the world could provide. Microsoft's investment ensured that OpenAI would have unrestricted access to Azure's most powerful AI-optimized infrastructure, a crucial advantage in an industry where computational limits often dictated the pace of progress.

But Microsoft's interest in OpenAI wasn't purely altruistic. The company had been searching for a way to regain its technological dominance after falling behind competitors like Google and Amazon in the AI race. By aligning itself with OpenAI, Microsoft positioned itself as a leader in AI-powered enterprise solutions. The partnership allowed Microsoft to integrate OpenAI's technology into its suite of products, enhancing everything from its cloud services to Office applications. Features like AI-assisted writing in Microsoft Word, intelligent search in Bing, and automated customer service chatbots all bore OpenAI's fingerprints.

Then came the game-changing moment: the 2023 multi-billion-dollar investment deal. By this time,

OpenAI had become a global phenomenon, and Microsoft saw an opportunity to deepen its control over what was becoming the most influential AI technology of the decade. Microsoft poured another $10 billion into OpenAI, effectively securing its place as OpenAI's primary backer. The deal transformed OpenAI from an independent research lab into a de facto Microsoft extension, albeit one that still retained some operational independence.

With this influx of funding and resources, OpenAI accelerated its development, leading to the launch of GPT-4 and the integration of AI assistants directly into Microsoft's ecosystem. The move was strategic—while companies like Google were racing to push their own AI chatbots into the market, Microsoft had effectively cornered the AI space by ensuring that OpenAI's most powerful models were deeply embedded in everyday tools used by businesses and consumers alike.

However, with power came responsibility, and Microsoft soon found itself in an uncomfortable position. OpenAI's dominance in the AI industry meant that any security vulnerabilities, data breaches, or ethical concerns associated with its models would reflect back on Microsoft. Regulators began scrutinizing the AI giant, questioning whether such an intimate partnership between a single company and one of the world's most advanced AI labs created an unfair monopoly on intelligence.

As OpenAI continued to grow under Microsoft's wing, it appeared almost invincible—until an unexpected challenger disrupted the landscape. DeepSeek, a relatively unknown Chinese AI startup, suddenly emerged with a model that claimed to rival OpenAI's technology, and it did so at a fraction of the cost. But as DeepSeek's rise shook the industry, Microsoft discovered something even more alarming: traces of suspicious activity that suggested OpenAI's technology might not have been as exclusive as they once thought. The AI war was no longer just about innovation—it was about security, secrecy, and survival.

As OpenAI surged ahead in the AI revolution, the rest of the tech world wasn't standing still. The sudden explosion of artificial intelligence ignited an arms race among the biggest players in the industry, with Google, Meta, Amazon, and a host of other companies pouring billions into AI research to ensure they weren't left behind.

Google, long regarded as the leader in machine learning thanks to its pioneering work in deep learning and natural language processing, had been working on its own AI advancements for years. Its research division, DeepMind, had already made headlines with AlphaGo, the AI system that defeated the world's best human Go player in 2016, and AlphaFold, which cracked one of biology's greatest mysteries by predicting protein structures with astonishing accuracy. But while Google's AI had achieved significant breakthroughs, it wasn't until OpenAI launched ChatGPT that the company realized it needed to move faster.

Caught off guard by the sudden rise of OpenAI's chatbot, Google rushed to push its own AI-powered language model, Bard, into the market. Unlike OpenAI, which had built a product-first approach by integrating GPT into apps and services, Google had kept much of its AI research confined to academic papers and experimental projects. Now, it had no choice but to accelerate deployment, integrating AI into its search engine and productivity tools to prevent Microsoft—fueled by its deep partnership with OpenAI—from gaining the upper hand.

Meanwhile, Meta had its own vision for the future of AI. Unlike OpenAI and Google, which pursued closed, proprietary AI models, Meta embraced open-source AI, making its LLaMA (Large Language Model Meta AI) series publicly available. This decision sparked an ongoing debate within the AI community: should the most powerful AI models be locked behind corporate walls, or should they be freely available for the world to build upon? Meta's bet was that by giving developers access to high-quality AI, it could create an ecosystem that would rival even OpenAI's dominance.

But building state-of-the-art AI models required more than just innovative algorithms—it required unprecedented amounts of computing power, data, and financial investment. Training models like GPT-4 or Google's Gemini wasn't just a research challenge; it was a resource war.

The cost of AI dominance quickly skyrocketed into the billions. Training GPT-4 alone was rumored to have cost OpenAI over $100 million, requiring access to thousands of Nvidia's H100 GPUs, the most powerful AI chips available. Google, Microsoft, and Meta all raced to secure these chips, leading to supply shortages that sent GPU prices soaring. AI companies found themselves in a fierce battle, not just against each other, but against the physical limitations of computing infrastructure.

Every new AI breakthrough required more power, more storage, and more engineering talent than ever before. Cloud computing giants like Microsoft Azure, Google Cloud, and Amazon Web Services became indispensable players in the AI race, as companies relied on their vast networks of data centers to train and run their models. The scale of investment required to compete in AI meant that only a handful of corporations had the resources to stay in the game, further consolidating power in the hands of a few tech giants.

But just as the world assumed that only the wealthiest, most established companies could build cutting-edge AI, a new player entered the scene. DeepSeek, a small startup from China, claimed it had developed an AI model that could match OpenAI's capabilities while spending a fraction of the cost. The numbers didn't seem to add up. How could a relatively unknown company achieve what had taken OpenAI, Google, and Microsoft billions of dollars and years of effort?

The answer, some speculated, lay not in innovation—but in access to OpenAI's intellectual property. As whispers of potential data theft and security breaches began to surface, the AI race took on a new dimension. It was no longer just about building the best model—it was about protecting secrets, securing technological advantages, and, for some, uncovering whether DeepSeek had cracked the code to outmaneuver Silicon Valley's biggest players.

Chapter 2: The Sudden Arrival of DeepSeek – Innovation or Imitation?

The world of artificial intelligence had been dominated by a handful of powerful players, each with the resources, talent, and infrastructure to push the limits of machine learning. Companies like OpenAI, Google, and Microsoft had spent billions developing AI models that required massive computing power and cutting-edge research. No one expected that an unknown startup from China, with no major public presence and no history of competing in the AI space, would suddenly emerge as a serious contender. But then, DeepSeek arrived.

For most of the world, the name DeepSeek meant nothing. Unlike OpenAI, which had built a reputation through years of research publications, industry collaborations, and high-profile AI launches, DeepSeek seemed to appear out of nowhere. There were no major announcements leading up to its debut, no slow buildup of hype—just the sudden release of a product so powerful that it forced the AI industry to take notice.

The breakthrough came in the form of DeepSeek R1, a large language model that seemed to perform at a level shockingly close to OpenAI's most advanced models. Unlike other AI startups that had struggled to reach even a fraction of OpenAI's capabilities, DeepSeek's chatbot demonstrated strong reasoning skills, impressive fluency in multiple languages, and a level of performance that rivaled the best AI models on the market. Almost overnight, DeepSeek's AI assistant became the number one free app on Apple's App Store in the United States, beating out ChatGPT and other AI competitors.

The numbers were staggering. In a matter of weeks, DeepSeek R1 climbed the charts in over fifty countries, drawing millions of users who were eager to test its capabilities. It wasn't just that DeepSeek had built a functioning chatbot—it had built a model that performed on par with OpenAI's best efforts, despite spending only a fraction of what OpenAI had invested in training its models.

For AI researchers and industry insiders, this raised serious questions. How had DeepSeek achieved this so quickly? Large-scale AI models weren't something that could be built overnight. They required vast datasets, immense computational resources, and years of iterative development. OpenAI's GPT-4 had taken years to refine, and Google's Gemini models were still struggling to match its capabilities. Yet DeepSeek, a company that had never been on anyone's radar, had suddenly built an AI that seemed to rival them all.

The startup itself remained quiet about the specifics of its technology. In its research paper, DeepSeek claimed that its model had been trained using only 2,000 Nvidia H800 GPUs and a budget of around $5.6 million—a tiny fraction of what OpenAI had spent to develop GPT-4. If these numbers were accurate, it would mean that DeepSeek had cracked the secret to building world-class AI at an efficiency that no one else had achieved.

Skepticism spread quickly. Prominent figures in the AI industry, including Palmer Luckey, the founder of Oculus VR, openly dismissed DeepSeek's claims, calling them bogus and Chinese propaganda designed to shake confidence in American tech. Elon Musk, who had been vocal about AI security risks, expressed his doubts as well, stating that it was "obvious" that DeepSeek must have had hidden access to advanced hardware or proprietary knowledge. Others speculated that DeepSeek might have quietly acquired data or techniques from OpenAI, allowing it to leapfrog the competition without having to invest the same level of resources.

Regardless of the speculation, one thing was clear: DeepSeek was a serious player, and its arrival had sent shockwaves through the AI industry. The sudden success of DeepSeek R1 wasn't just about its performance—it was about the larger implications of a smaller, lesser-known company competing at the highest levels of artificial intelligence.

Was DeepSeek truly a revolutionary AI lab that had discovered a more efficient way to train and optimize AI models? Or had it taken a shortcut, gaining access to OpenAI's work through means that were, at best, questionable?

As the AI community scrambled for answers, Microsoft and OpenAI were already looking deeper into an even more disturbing possibility—one that would soon escalate into a full-scale investigation. Had DeepSeek actually stolen OpenAI's knowledge?

When DeepSeek R1 launched, few outside of China had even heard of the company behind it. Unlike OpenAI, which had spent years building its reputation as a pioneer in artificial intelligence, DeepSeek had no high-profile research papers, no partnerships with global tech giants, and no marketing campaigns teasing its arrival. And yet, within weeks of its debut, DeepSeek's AI assistant became the most downloaded free app on the Apple App Store in the United States and across more than fifty countries.

The rapid ascent of DeepSeek R1 was nothing short of stunning. Chatbots and AI-powered assistants had already flooded the market, and with OpenAI's ChatGPT dominating the space, breaking through seemed nearly impossible for any new competitor. But DeepSeek defied expectations. Its app didn't just gain traction—it overtook ChatGPT itself, drawing in millions of users seemingly overnight.

At first, industry analysts assumed the sudden surge was driven by novelty—people simply curious to test out a new AI model, much like they had when ChatGPT first launched. But as more users engaged with DeepSeek R1, it became clear that this was no ordinary chatbot.

For one, DeepSeek offered free and unrestricted access to its AI assistant, while OpenAI had begun placing more limitations on free-tier users, nudging them toward paid subscriptions for ChatGPT Plus. The removal of paywalls made DeepSeek instantly more attractive to casual users who wanted a full AI experience without restrictions.

But what really caught the industry's attention was the model's sheer capability. Early tests showed that DeepSeek R1 could handle complex reasoning, creative writing, and even mathematical challenges with a level of proficiency that put it in the same league as OpenAI's latest models. In some cases, it even outperformed ChatGPT, particularly in tasks that required retrieving specific factual information.

Users marveled at its responsiveness, fluency, and ability to generate well-structured answers across a wide range of topics. Unlike many rushed AI releases that suffered from glaring inconsistencies or poor language coherence, DeepSeek R1 felt polished—almost too polished for a company that had seemingly appeared out of nowhere.

The explosive growth of DeepSeek's app quickly raised eyebrows within the AI community. How had this startup managed to attract millions of users so quickly? Some suspected aggressive marketing tactics, but there was little evidence of traditional advertising behind its viral success. The momentum appeared to be entirely organic, fueled by word-of-mouth and user curiosity.

Then came the more troubling questions: If DeepSeek had truly built this model from scratch, why hadn't there been any signs of its development before? Building a competitive AI model typically required years of training, massive datasets, and extensive fine-tuning. Yet DeepSeek's model had materialized seemingly out of thin air, ready to challenge the best AI systems in the world.

The numbers also didn't add up. OpenAI's ChatGPT had been trained on vast resources, with a budget that reportedly exceeded $100 million, supported by 25,000 of Nvidia's cutting-edge H100 GPUs. DeepSeek, by contrast, claimed to have built R1 using just 2,000 H800 GPUs—a fraction of the cost. If that was true, it meant that DeepSeek had discovered a way to train AI models with an efficiency that no one else had achieved.

Skepticism spread. Some experts pointed out that DeepSeek's AI seemed eerily familiar—too similar, in fact, to OpenAI's technology. Had DeepSeek somehow gained access to OpenAI's model architecture, training methods, or even its proprietary datasets? Microsoft's security teams, closely monitoring OpenAI's systems, soon reported unusual activity tied to DeepSeek.

What had started as a shocking success story was now morphing into something much bigger. DeepSeek's meteoric rise wasn't just disrupting the AI market—it was triggering an intense investigation into whether its success had come from innovation or something far more controversial.

DeepSeek's sudden rise from obscurity to dominance in the AI space was nothing short of unbelievable. While OpenAI had spent years developing its large language models with billions in funding and some of the world's most advanced computing resources, DeepSeek—a previously unknown Chinese startup—had seemingly matched OpenAI's performance with a fraction of the budget and infrastructure.

Naturally, this raised serious questions. How had a company that wasn't even on the industry's radar just months before suddenly built an AI that could go head-to-head with GPT-4? If DeepSeek's claims about its training process were true, it had done something unprecedented—achieving OpenAI-level performance at an efficiency no one else had mastered. But if the claims were false, the explanation for its success might be far more controversial.

Industry insiders and AI researchers immediately began scrutinizing DeepSeek's numbers. The startup claimed it had trained its R1 model on just 2,000 Nvidia H800 GPUs, costing only $5.6 million. By contrast, OpenAI's GPT-4 was rumored to have required over 25,000 H100 GPUs, with a training cost exceeding $100 million. Even Google, with its vast resources, had struggled to match OpenAI's efficiency. Yet here was DeepSeek, a company with no track record in AI research, claiming to have built an equally powerful model on a shoestring budget.

It didn't take long for skepticism to spread. Palmer Luckey, the founder of Oculus VR and a vocal figure in the AI community, publicly dismissed DeepSeek's claims, calling them "bogus" and suggesting that the startup's success was part of a strategic misinformation campaign. Others speculated that DeepSeek had secretly gained access to far more powerful hardware than it had disclosed, possibly acquiring thousands of high-end GPUs through undisclosed channels.

Some experts proposed another possibility: Was DeepSeek simply repackaging OpenAI's work? AI model distillation—a technique where a smaller model learns by imitating the outputs of a larger, more powerful one—was a well-known method in the industry. If DeepSeek had managed to extract knowledge from OpenAI's API or research papers, it could have effectively compressed OpenAI's expertise into its own system, producing similar results without needing the same level of computational power.

Even more concerning were the whispers that DeepSeek's rise wasn't just a story of clever engineering—it was a case of corporate espionage. According to reports from Microsoft's security teams, anomalous activity had been detected within OpenAI's API months before DeepSeek's launch. Certain entities, allegedly linked to DeepSeek, had been pulling vast amounts of data from OpenAI's system, raising the possibility that DeepSeek had systematically extracted OpenAI's model outputs to train its own AI.

Elon Musk, never one to stay silent on AI controversies, weighed in with his own doubts. When one user on social media suggested that DeepSeek must have had hidden access to advanced computing hardware, Musk simply replied, "Obviously." Meanwhile, Alexander Wang, the CEO of Scale AI, speculated that DeepSeek had secretly acquired access to tens of thousands of high-end GPUs, possibly circumventing U.S. chip restrictions.

But even as skepticism grew, DeepSeek remained largely silent. The company did little to clarify its methods or defend itself against accusations, offering only a vague research paper that left many questions unanswered. The AI community remained divided—was DeepSeek truly a breakthrough in AI efficiency, or had it taken a shortcut that no one else was willing to admit?

One thing was certain: DeepSeek's rise had triggered an industry-wide panic. OpenAI, Google, and Microsoft had all assumed that AI dominance would belong to those with the most computing power, the most talent, and the most funding. But if DeepSeek's model was legitimate, it rewrote the rules of the AI game—proving that a well-engineered system could potentially rival billion-dollar corporations without requiring the same level of investment.

However, if the more sinister theories were true—if DeepSeek had stolen intellectual property, siphoned data from OpenAI, or leveraged undisclosed resources—then this wasn't just a technological breakthrough. It was an act of AI warfare.

The industry was left waiting for answers, but one thing was clear: DeepSeek's success wasn't just a business story anymore—it was a geopolitical and economic flashpoint that could reshape the global AI race.

Chapter 3: The Stolen Tech Allegations – Fact or Fiction?

As DeepSeek's unexpected success continued to rattle the AI industry, Microsoft's security team made a troubling discovery. While reviewing OpenAI's systems, investigators detected unusual activity tied to DeepSeek—patterns that suggested large-scale data extraction from OpenAI's API.

OpenAI's API was designed to provide external developers access to its language models, allowing businesses to integrate AI capabilities into their applications. These developers paid for API usage, sending prompts to OpenAI's models and receiving responses in return. But something about this activity didn't add up. Over a period of several months, massive amounts of requests had been made from sources linked to DeepSeek, far exceeding typical usage patterns.

At first, it wasn't clear what this meant. AI models naturally improve as they interact with more queries, but the volume of data being accessed suggested something beyond normal development. Microsoft's security researchers, who had a vested interest in OpenAI's operations due to their multi-billion-dollar investment, flagged the activity as a potential security breach.

The theory that quickly emerged was one that sent shockwaves through OpenAI's leadership: Had DeepSeek used OpenAI's API to systematically extract model outputs and train its own AI?

This process, known as distillation, wasn't new. In AI research, distillation is a technique where a smaller or less powerful model is trained by learning from the outputs of a larger, more advanced model. Instead of requiring access to the original model's internal architecture or training data, a company could simply observe how the model responds to different prompts and then fine-tune its own system to mimic those responses.

At its core, distillation works by feeding a model millions of questions and recording the answers given by a superior AI system. The student model then generalizes from this data, gradually absorbing the knowledge and decision-making patterns of its teacher. Done at scale, distillation could allow a competitor to replicate key aspects of OpenAI's intelligence without having direct access to its proprietary code or datasets.

For OpenAI, this was a nightmare scenario. If DeepSeek had indeed used distillation—not by studying publicly available research, but by pulling knowledge directly from OpenAI's API—then it had effectively reverse-engineered OpenAI's intelligence without violating traditional cybersecurity measures. No hacking, no breach of internal servers—just an aggressive, systematic siphoning of OpenAI's intelligence through the very API that was meant to generate revenue.

The implications were staggering. If DeepSeek had indeed leveraged this technique, it meant that a billion-dollar AI advantage could be compressed into a few months of large-scale API querying. OpenAI had spent years and hundreds of millions of dollars training its models, fine-tuning them with human feedback, and improving their reasoning capabilities. If DeepSeek had managed to clone those capabilities at a fraction of the cost, it would be one of the most audacious moves in AI history—a heist without breaking any doors.

As word of Microsoft's investigation spread, the AI community became increasingly divided. Some argued that distillation, while controversial, wasn't inherently theft—after all, if an AI model generates public outputs, what's stopping another company from learning from them? Others insisted that what DeepSeek had done—if the allegations were true—was no different from stealing trade secrets.

Meanwhile, OpenAI and Microsoft remained tight-lipped, refusing to release further details about their findings. But one thing was certain: if DeepSeek had really built its AI on the backbone of

OpenAI's knowledge, then this wasn't just a case of corporate rivalry—it was an existential threat to OpenAI's entire business model.

The battle lines were drawn. The question now wasn't just whether DeepSeek had used distillation—it was whether it had done so legally, ethically, and at a scale that could permanently change the AI industry.

As the AI world scrambled to make sense of DeepSeek's meteoric rise, some of the most influential voices in tech and security raised serious concerns about how the Chinese startup had managed to achieve such a breakthrough. Among them was David Sachs, a prominent investor and entrepreneur with deep ties to both AI and cybersecurity. Sachs, along with other AI security experts, wasn't convinced that DeepSeek's success had been purely the result of innovation. Instead, he suggested something far more troubling: DeepSeek had extracted OpenAI's knowledge and compressed it into its own model.

The theory wasn't just based on speculation. Sachs pointed to substantial evidence that DeepSeek had engaged in a sophisticated operation to absorb OpenAI's intelligence without direct access to its internal research. This wasn't a case of stolen code or leaked blueprints—it was a methodical process that leveraged OpenAI's own publicly available API to replicate its capabilities.

Sachs and other security experts described it as a form of AI replication that blurred the line between fair competition and intellectual property theft. DeepSeek, they argued, had likely spent months—possibly years—systematically querying OpenAI's API at a massive scale. By feeding its own training pipeline with GPT-generated responses, it could have reverse-engineered OpenAI's intelligence, distilling its essence into a new model.

The problem, however, was proving it. AI models don't leave fingerprints. If a company copies software code or steals internal data, there's a clear trail. But AI knowledge—especially when extracted through an API—is more elusive. DeepSeek wouldn't have needed access to OpenAI's training datasets or model architecture. It only needed access to the outputs. By analyzing millions of responses from OpenAI's most advanced models, it could have trained its own system to mimic the same reasoning patterns, linguistic structures, and problem-solving capabilities.

For OpenAI and Microsoft, this was a dangerous precedent. If DeepSeek had pulled this off, what stopped other companies from doing the same? Could any competitor, with enough time and API access, simply absorb the knowledge of the world's most advanced AI models and repackage it as their own?

The allegations raised an even bigger question: Did OpenAI's business model have a fundamental flaw? If OpenAI's API could be used as a training set for competitors, it meant that every response it generated was, in effect, a knowledge leak. Sachs and other experts argued that OpenAI had inadvertently made its own intelligence vulnerable—by offering access to its AI through a public API, it had provided a backdoor for competitors to absorb its breakthroughs.

The implications of this discovery were far-reaching. If DeepSeek had truly built a near-GPT-4 level AI using OpenAI's own knowledge, then the race for AI supremacy had just taken a dramatic turn. The competition was no longer just about who could build the best models—it was about who could extract knowledge the fastest.

Despite growing concerns, DeepSeek remained silent. The company issued no public statements addressing the allegations. Meanwhile, OpenAI and Microsoft intensified their investigation, searching for any concrete proof that DeepSeek had siphoned their knowledge. But the challenge remained: how do you prove that an AI model was trained on another AI model's responses?

With no direct evidence yet released, the tech world was left to speculate. Had DeepSeek truly outsmarted OpenAI, or had it simply found a way to bypass the barriers of traditional AI research and cut straight to the finished product?

One thing was certain—if DeepSeek had done it, others would follow. And the entire AI industry was now watching closely to see if OpenAI would find a way to fight back.

Artificial intelligence distillation is a controversial yet widely used technique that allows a smaller or less complex AI model to learn from the outputs of a more advanced one. At its core, distillation is a process of compression—taking a large, highly trained AI and using its responses to train a more efficient, often smaller model that mimics its capabilities. This method isn't inherently illegal, nor is it new. It has been used for years in AI research to refine models, reduce computing costs, and make AI systems more efficient. But in the case of DeepSeek and OpenAI, the situation was far more complicated.

At its most basic level, AI distillation works by feeding a student model millions of queries and capturing the responses of a larger, more capable teacher model. Over time, the student learns to generalize these patterns, effectively replicating the knowledge and decision-making processes of its teacher. The advantage of this approach is that it allows companies to develop high-performing AI systems without needing to train them entirely from scratch—a process that can take years and require hundreds of millions of dollars in computing resources.

The ethical and legal dilemma arises when distillation is used in a way that replicates proprietary knowledge without authorization. If a company were to systematically extract intelligence from a competitor's AI model—especially one that is behind a paid API or part of a private research lab—it would raise serious questions about intellectual property rights. Was this a form of reverse engineering, a legitimate method of AI development, or outright theft?

In traditional software development, reverse engineering is a gray area. It involves deconstructing a competitor's product to understand how it works, often with the goal of recreating similar functionality. In many industries, this is a legally accepted practice as long as no direct copying of proprietary code or data occurs. Companies study competitors' products all the time, analyzing features, performance, and structure to improve their own offerings. However, when reverse engineering involves copying trade secrets or circumventing intellectual property protections, it crosses into illegal territory.

With AI, the situation is even more complex. AI models don't have source code in the same way traditional software does. Instead, they operate as massive neural networks trained on vast datasets. If one company's model learns by observing the outputs of another company's AI, can that be considered theft? Or is it simply an accelerated form of learning?

In the case of DeepSeek, the scale and intent behind the alleged distillation were key factors. If DeepSeek had simply trained its AI on publicly available data, such as open-source models, research papers, or publicly accessible chatbot interactions, it would have been seen as fair competition—an efficient and strategic use of available resources. But if the company had intentionally extracted vast amounts of data from OpenAI's API, effectively absorbing its decision-making patterns to build an equivalent model, it would be far closer to intellectual property theft than simple imitation.

The stakes in this debate were enormous. If DeepSeek's methods were accepted as fair game, it would set a precedent that any AI company could extract knowledge from its competitors without legal consequences. OpenAI and Microsoft, both heavily invested in AI security, had a vested interest in ensuring that this didn't happen. If DeepSeek had truly leveraged OpenAI's work to leapfrog ahead, it wasn't just a business rivalry anymore—it was a battle over the fundamental rules of AI development in the modern era.

The broader AI industry was divided. Some saw DeepSeek's approach as an inevitable evolution of AI research, arguing that knowledge transfer had always been a key part of technological progress. Others saw it as a dangerous loophole, one that could render proprietary AI research meaningless if companies could simply extract intelligence from existing systems instead of investing in their own breakthroughs.

Ultimately, the case of DeepSeek forced a larger question into the spotlight: In an industry built on data, knowledge, and open research, where do we draw the line between inspiration, replication, and theft? And if AI models were capable of learning from each other, was it even possible to regulate the exchange of intelligence in a way that protected innovation without stifling progress?

As OpenAI and Microsoft ramped up their investigation, the world was watching closely. What was at stake wasn't just the future of one company, but the entire framework of competition and ethics in artificial intelligence.

Chapter 4: The Numbers That Didn't Add Up

DeepSeek's rise to prominence was shocking enough, but what truly sent waves through the AI industry was its claim that it had developed a model rivaling OpenAI's most advanced AI with just $5.6 million.

For context, OpenAI's GPT-4 was widely believed to have cost well over $100 million to train, requiring an estimated 25,000 Nvidia H100 GPUs—some of the most powerful and expensive AI chips in existence. By contrast, DeepSeek claimed to have built its own cutting-edge model, DeepSeek R1, with only 2,000 Nvidia H800 GPUs—a fraction of OpenAI's resources. If these numbers were accurate, it meant DeepSeek had achieved something no other AI company had—creating a world-class model on a budget that seemed almost impossible.

At first, industry insiders assumed there had to be a mistake. Training a high-performance AI model required three key components: enormous datasets, massive computational power, and years of research. Even companies with deep pockets, like Google and Meta, struggled to match OpenAI's advancements, despite investing billions. Yet here was DeepSeek, a startup with no known breakthroughs, claiming it had cracked the code to AI efficiency.

Skepticism spread quickly. How had DeepSeek accomplished what even the most well-funded AI labs had not?

The most immediate theory was that DeepSeek had developed a radically more efficient training process—perhaps one that optimized GPU usage to a degree that no one else had achieved. But AI researchers quickly dismissed this idea. While incremental improvements in efficiency were possible, no known method could reduce training costs by such an extreme margin while maintaining state-of-the-art performance.

Then came a more controversial explanation: Had DeepSeek cut costs by training its AI on OpenAI's outputs?

If DeepSeek had leveraged AI distillation, systematically extracting data from OpenAI's API and using it to train its own model, it would have dramatically reduced the amount of raw computing power required to build an equivalent system. Rather than spending millions of dollars refining its model with trial and error, it could have directly learned from OpenAI's decision-making processes, effectively bypassing much of the training phase.

The numbers started to make more sense under this theory. If DeepSeek had access to vast amounts of high-quality AI-generated text from OpenAI's API, it could have used those responses to shortcut the need for the same level of computing power. Instead of training from scratch, it would have trained its AI to mimic the reasoning and response patterns of GPT-4—an approach that would have been significantly cheaper than OpenAI's full-scale development process.

But if this was true, DeepSeek's success was not just a breakthrough in efficiency—it was a direct challenge to the business model of OpenAI and other AI giants. If a startup could replicate cutting-edge AI models with a fraction of the cost by distilling their outputs, what stopped other competitors from doing the same?

The implications were massive. OpenAI's high-cost, high-performance approach depended on keeping its models ahead of the competition. But if DeepSeek's methods were legitimate—or at least impossible to regulate—then every AI company in the world would be forced to rethink its strategy.

Some industry leaders dismissed DeepSeek's claims outright. Palmer Luckey, the founder of Oculus VR, called DeepSeek's cost estimates "bogus," suggesting that its numbers were deliberately misleading to create hype. Others, like **Alexander

Wang, CEO of Scale AI, speculated that DeepSeek must have had access to far more GPUs than it admitted, possibly acquiring tens of thousands of high-end chips through undisclosed sources.

Regardless of how it had been achieved, one thing was clear: DeepSeek's claim of building a GPT-4-level AI for just $5.6 million was either a groundbreaking efficiency breakthrough—or the result of methods that OpenAI and Microsoft would consider highly questionable.

As investigations continued, the AI world remained on edge. If DeepSeek had truly discovered a way to build AI models at a fraction of the usual cost, it would change the economics of artificial intelligence forever. But if it had taken shortcuts by siphoning OpenAI's knowledge, it was only a matter of time before Microsoft and OpenAI took action.

One of the most baffling aspects of DeepSeek's rise was its claim that it had built a GPT-4-level AI model using only 2,000 Nvidia H800 GPUs. By comparison, OpenAI had reportedly required 25,000 H100 GPUs to train GPT-4—an order of magnitude more in terms of raw computing power. If DeepSeek's numbers were accurate, it had achieved a level of efficiency that defied industry expectations.

For those familiar with AI model training, the discrepancy was staggering. GPUs are the backbone of artificial intelligence development. Training a large language model requires millions of processing cycles to analyze and refine massive datasets. The more powerful the hardware, the faster and more capable the AI model becomes. Nvidia's H100 GPUs were considered the gold standard, used by nearly every major AI lab due to their unparalleled speed, memory, and ability to handle large-scale deep learning tasks.

By contrast, DeepSeek's reported use of H800 GPUs raised serious questions. While the H800 was still a powerful AI chip, it was designed as a downgraded version of the H100, specifically made to comply with U.S. export restrictions on advanced computing hardware to China. The H800 had lower performance limits in terms of communication bandwidth and processing speed, making it less efficient for large-scale AI training.

So how had DeepSeek managed to match OpenAI's performance with so much less computing power?

Industry experts proposed several theories.

The first theory was that DeepSeek had developed a radically optimized training process that allowed it to squeeze more performance out of fewer GPUs. While possible, this explanation seemed unlikely. Companies like OpenAI, Google, and Meta had already pushed GPU efficiency to the limit, using techniques like distributed training, mixed-precision computing, and reinforcement learning optimizations. The idea that DeepSeek had discovered a game-changing efficiency technique that no one else had was hard to believe.

The second theory was that DeepSeek had secretly used far more hardware than it admitted. Some analysts speculated that DeepSeek may have had access to additional Nvidia GPUs through undisclosed sources, potentially operating training clusters beyond what it publicly reported. If DeepSeek had managed to acquire thousands of extra H100 GPUs through unofficial channels, it could have significantly boosted its AI training capacity without drawing attention.

A third, more controversial theory was that DeepSeek had sidestepped the need for massive computational resources by leveraging OpenAI's own model outputs. If DeepSeek had used AI distillation—training its model based on ChatGPT's responses rather than training from scratch—it would have dramatically reduced the amount of raw computing power needed. Instead of performing all the complex calculations itself, DeepSeek could have "learned" from GPT-4's outputs, bypassing much of the expensive computational process.

Adding to the mystery was the geopolitical element. The U.S. had placed strict export restrictions on Nvidia's most powerful AI chips, including the H100, precisely to prevent China from advancing too quickly in AI. If DeepSeek had still managed to train an advanced model despite these restrictions, it raised serious questions about China's ability to work around U.S. chip bans.

Some experts pointed to Huawei's involvement in AI chip production. While DeepSeek had reportedly used Nvidia GPUs for training, Huawei's Ascend 910C chips were believed to be used for running the model (also known as inference). Could DeepSeek have combined multiple sources of hardware to get around its limitations? If so, it meant that China's AI industry was finding ways to stay competitive despite the West's attempts to cut off its access to critical hardware.

At the end of the day, there was no clear answer to how DeepSeek had achieved what it claimed with such limited resources. Either the company had discovered a revolutionary AI training efficiency breakthrough, acquired additional hardware in secret, or used alternative methods—possibly OpenAI's own intelligence—to compensate for the lack of raw computing power.

The hardware puzzle wasn't just a question of technology—it was a question of whether DeepSeek's rise had been the result of true innovation or a well-executed shortcut. And as the investigation into DeepSeek's methods intensified, Microsoft and OpenAI were determined to find out the truth.

As DeepSeek's claims about its AI's efficiency spread, skepticism began pouring in from some of the most influential voices in the tech world. Among them were Palmer Luckey, the founder of Oculus VR and a key figure in defense and AI technology, and Elon Musk, the billionaire entrepreneur with deep investments in artificial intelligence. Both were openly doubtful that DeepSeek had legitimately built a GPT-4-level model with the limited resources it had publicly disclosed.

Palmer Luckey, known for his blunt takes on disruptive technology, was one of the first to publicly dismiss DeepSeek's numbers as "bogus." He suggested that the startup's claim of training a world-class AI model for just $5.6 million using only 2,000 H800 GPUs was mathematically impossible under conventional AI development constraints. He didn't just question their methods—he outright called the company's numbers fraudulent.

Elon Musk, never one to shy away from a controversy, quickly joined the conversation. When an X (formerly Twitter) user pointed out that DeepSeek must have had hidden access to more powerful hardware than it claimed, Musk responded with a single word: "Obviously." His comment fueled speculation that DeepSeek had been operating with resources far beyond what it was willing to admit.

The growing doubts led to one major question: Did DeepSeek secretly gain access to advanced computing resources?

For an AI model to perform at GPT-4's level, it required massive computational power, specialized hardware, and months—if not years—of iterative training. Yet DeepSeek claimed to have achieved this with a fraction of the GPUs and a fraction of the cost. The more analysts examined these numbers, the less they added up.

One theory was that DeepSeek had somehow acquired access to thousands of Nvidia's high-performance H100 GPUs, despite U.S. export restrictions on advanced chips to China.

Industry insiders pointed out that China had been aggressively acquiring AI hardware through indirect channels, with reports of companies stockpiling Nvidia chips before the bans took full effect. Some speculated that DeepSeek could have sourced additional hardware from private suppliers, bypassing regulatory restrictions and massively increasing its computing power. If DeepSeek had managed to secure tens of thousands of high-performance GPUs under the radar, it would explain how it had built a model far more powerful than its disclosed hardware should have allowed.

Another possibility was that DeepSeek had leveraged an alternative computing infrastructure. While Nvidia chips were the most sought-after AI accelerators, China had been developing its own domestic alternatives, such as Huawei's Ascend 910C chips. Some experts theorized that DeepSeek could have used a hybrid approach—training on Nvidia GPUs while deploying its model on Huawei chips for inference. If true, it would indicate that China's AI sector was adapting to U.S. chip bans far more effectively than anticipated.

But there was an even more unsettling theory: What if DeepSeek didn't need to train from scratch at all?

Palmer Luckey and other AI analysts speculated that DeepSeek might have found a way to shortcut the training process entirely—by using OpenAI's own intelligence as a foundation. If DeepSeek had extracted OpenAI's API data and applied AI distillation techniques, it could have dramatically reduced the amount of raw computing power required. Instead of building an AI from the ground up, it could have fine-tuned an existing model using OpenAI's outputs, effectively "cloning" the reasoning and linguistic patterns of GPT-4.

The possibility that DeepSeek had taken such a shortcut raised concerns not just about competition, but about intellectual property security in the AI race. If a company could reverse-engineer OpenAI's AI without ever accessing its internal code or datasets, what stopped other AI firms from doing the same?

Despite mounting pressure, DeepSeek remained silent on these accusations. The company released no public statements clarifying its resource usage, nor did it offer transparency about its model's development process. This silence only deepened suspicions.

As speculation swirled, Microsoft and OpenAI intensified their investigation, determined to uncover the truth. If DeepSeek had truly outmaneuvered OpenAI with a more efficient training process, it would mark a revolutionary breakthrough in AI development. But if it had secretly acquired undisclosed hardware or siphoned OpenAI's knowledge, it would set the stage for one of the biggest AI controversies in history.

With powerful voices like Luckey and Musk openly casting doubt, the pressure was on DeepSeek to prove that its rise wasn't built on deception. The question was: Would they be able to?

Chapter 5: The China Factor – AI, Geopolitics, and Technological Warfare

The rivalry between the United States and China has long extended beyond politics and economics, but in recent years, the battle for AI dominance has become one of the most critical frontlines in their ongoing technological war. Artificial intelligence isn't just about chatbots and automation—it's about control over the next era of military strategy, economic power, and global influence. The country that leads in AI will shape the world's future, from autonomous warfare and surveillance to financial markets and biotech innovation.

For years, the U.S. held a clear advantage in AI development, with Silicon Valley serving as the global hub for machine learning research. Companies like OpenAI, Google, Microsoft, and Meta were backed by massive amounts of venture capital, world-class engineers, and access to the most advanced semiconductor technology. The dominance of Nvidia's GPUs, particularly the high-powered H100 chips, gave American AI firms an almost unbeatable edge, as these chips were the backbone of training and running state-of-the-art AI models.

But China had been rapidly catching up. Over the past decade, Beijing had poured billions into AI research, fostering an ecosystem of companies like Alibaba, Baidu, and Tencent to develop their own large-scale models. The Chinese government recognized that AI was a strategic necessity, and rather than leaving development solely to private corporations, it positioned AI as a national priority, embedding it into military applications, economic strategies, and long-term national planning.

The speed at which China's AI sector grew alarmed Washington. Not only were Chinese firms advancing rapidly, but they were also integrating AI into surveillance technology, cyber warfare strategies, and state-controlled information networks. The idea of China surpassing the U.S. in

AI capabilities was no longer hypothetical—it was a real possibility.

In response, the United States took action. Washington implemented a series of aggressive export bans, targeting the very foundation of China's AI revolution—Nvidia's GPUs. The logic was simple: If China couldn't access the best AI chips, it wouldn't be able to train the most advanced AI models.

In October 2022, the U.S. Commerce Department announced sweeping restrictions on exporting high-end AI chips to China. This included cutting off China's access to Nvidia's A100 and H100 GPUs, which were essential for training large-scale AI models. The goal was to slow China's AI development by limiting its ability to train competitive systems while allowing U.S. companies to maintain their technological lead.

However, China adapted faster than expected. Nvidia responded by creating a downgraded version of its AI chips, the H800, specifically designed to comply with U.S. restrictions while still being legally exportable to China. While the H800 was weaker than the H100, it was still powerful enough to train sophisticated AI models—just at a higher cost and with longer training times.

But China wasn't just relying on modified Nvidia chips. Domestic semiconductor giants, like Huawei, stepped in to fill the gap. The company unveiled its Ascend 910C chips, which, while not as powerful as Nvidia's cutting-edge hardware, provided an alternative that Chinese AI firms could use to reduce dependence on American technology.

The U.S. soon realized that export restrictions alone wouldn't be enough to cripple China's AI ambitions. Despite limitations, Chinese companies continued to develop competitive AI models and sought out alternative supply chains to acquire high-performance chips. Reports emerged that Chinese AI firms were buying thousands of Nvidia chips through third-party countries, bypassing U.S. sanctions.

Then came DeepSeek.

The sudden emergence of DeepSeek R1, a GPT-4-level AI model built with only 2,000 H800 GPUs, sent shockwaves through the industry. If DeepSeek had truly managed to train an AI without access to America's most advanced computing hardware, it meant that China had already found a way to sidestep U.S. restrictions.

For Washington, this was a red flag. It signaled that China's AI industry was far more resilient than previously thought. If DeepSeek could build world-class AI despite chip bans, what else was China capable of developing?

The U.S.-China AI arms race was no longer just a battle of corporations. It was a geopolitical struggle with global consequences. America's strategy had been built around cutting off China's access to AI chips, but DeepSeek's success suggested that China was already finding ways to adapt.

The bigger question was: Would the U.S. tighten restrictions even further? And if China had already found ways to work around them, was it even possible to contain its rise in AI supremacy?

As DeepSeek's model continued to gain traction, it wasn't just OpenAI and Microsoft that were watching—it was the entire U.S. intelligence community. Because if DeepSeek had truly built this AI against all odds, it meant the AI war had only just begun.

As the United States tightened its grip on AI chip exports, China's tech industry found itself in a race against time. The loss of access to Nvidia's high-performance H100 and A100 GPUs—critical for training advanced AI models—threatened to derail the country's artificial intelligence ambitions. But rather than slowing down, China adapted with remarkable speed, finding ways to keep its AI development on track despite U.S. restrictions.

At the heart of China's counter-strategy was Huawei's Ascend 910C, a domestically developed AI chip that became a crucial alternative to Nvidia's cutting-edge processors. While the Ascend 910C wasn't as powerful as the H100, it provided just enough computing power to keep Chinese AI firms competitive, particularly in the area of inference—where trained models process user queries rather than undergoing intensive training.

Huawei's efforts to reduce China's reliance on Western AI hardware weren't new. The company had been developing AI accelerators for years, anticipating that increasing U.S. restrictions would eventually cut off access to Nvidia and other American tech giants. The original Ascend 910, released in 2019, had already been used for AI research within China, but the newer 910C model was designed specifically to bridge the performance gap left by the loss of Nvidia's chips.

Although the H100 still outperformed the Ascend 910C in raw power, Chinese engineers found creative ways to work around the limitations. Instead of training models entirely on Chinese chips, many AI firms adopted a hybrid strategy—using the limited supply of Nvidia GPUs they had acquired before the bans for the heavy lifting, while deploying the Ascend 910C for inference and smaller-scale AI tasks. This approach allowed companies like Alibaba, Baidu, and DeepSeek to continue scaling AI development despite Washington's efforts to slow them down.

Huawei, meanwhile, positioned itself as a savior for China's AI industry. The company ramped up production of the Ascend 910C, marketing it as a viable alternative to Nvidia's hardware. Government-backed AI projects within China shifted their focus toward domestic chip solutions, investing heavily in semiconductor manufacturing to ensure that future AI research wouldn't be crippled by U.S. trade restrictions.

For firms like DeepSeek, the rise of Huawei's AI hardware was a lifeline. While DeepSeek still relied on Nvidia's H800 chips for training, it reportedly used Huawei's Ascend 910C for inference—allowing it to deploy its AI assistant at scale without relying on restricted Western hardware. If DeepSeek's model truly ran efficiently on Chinese-built chips, it suggested that China's AI sector was becoming increasingly self-sufficient, undermining Washington's export bans.

This shift carried massive geopolitical implications. The U.S. had assumed that blocking Nvidia's AI chips would delay China's AI progress by years. But the success of DeepSeek and the wider adoption of Huawei's Ascend 910C suggested otherwise. China was finding ways to adapt—and fast.

The question now was whether Huawei and other Chinese semiconductor firms could further close the gap with American hardware. If they succeeded, it would permanently alter the balance of power in AI development, proving that even the most aggressive trade restrictions couldn't stop China's technological rise.

DeepSeek's breakthrough was just the beginning. The arms race in AI wasn't just about models—it was about the silicon that powered them. And if China could produce its own high-performance AI chips at scale, the U.S. would need to rethink its entire strategy for maintaining technological supremacy.

The rise of DeepSeek and China's ability to push forward in AI development despite strict U.S. trade restrictions sent shockwaves through the global tech industry. For years, Washington had operated under the assumption that controlling access to advanced AI chips—particularly Nvidia's H100 and A100—would slow down China's progress. But DeepSeek's breakthrough, combined with the country's rapid adaptation to domestic alternatives like Huawei's Ascend 910C, suggested a different reality: China wasn't just surviving AI restrictions—it was possibly outpacing the U.S. in key areas.

This realization triggered immediate panic on Wall Street and in Silicon Valley. Investors had long viewed American AI giants—OpenAI, Microsoft, Google, and Nvidia—as the undisputed leaders of artificial intelligence. But if DeepSeek's technology was truly competitive with OpenAI's, it meant that the AI advantage was no longer exclusively in American hands.

The market reacted with unprecedented volatility. DeepSeek's sudden rise and the broader fear of China's acceleration in AI wiped out $600 billion in Nvidia's market cap in a single day—the biggest single-day loss in U.S. stock market history. Investors, once confident in Nvidia's stranglehold on the AI hardware market, began fearing that China was on the verge of self-sufficiency in AI chips and software.

Beyond Nvidia, other tech giants saw their valuations take a hit. If China could develop world-class AI models without relying on U.S. companies, then OpenAI, Google, and Meta faced a serious long-term threat. Microsoft, which had invested billions into OpenAI, scrambled to assess how DeepSeek's success could affect its dominance in the AI space.

At the same time, the U.S. government was forced to confront a difficult truth: Had AI restrictions backfired? By limiting China's access to high-performance chips, Washington had hoped to cripple its AI sector, but instead, China had been forced to innovate and accelerate its domestic semiconductor efforts. Now, it appeared that these restrictions had done little to stop the country's momentum—and in some cases, they had possibly pushed China to become more self-reliant.

If China could develop AI models that rivaled OpenAI's best work without access to Nvidia's cutting-edge hardware, what did that mean for the future of U.S. technological dominance? Would America's AI industry remain the global leader, or would it soon find itself outpaced by a nation that had learned to work around every barrier?

DeepSeek's rise wasn't just a challenge to OpenAI—it was a wake-up call to the entire Western AI ecosystem. The AI arms race was no longer a competition between Silicon Valley's biggest players—it was now a full-scale geopolitical struggle with no clear winner in sight.

Chapter 6: Alibaba Enters the Arena – The AI Wars Escalate

The AI landscape had barely caught its breath from DeepSeek's shock entry when Alibaba made its move. While OpenAI had long dominated the global AI scene and DeepSeek had turned heads with its unexpectedly powerful model, Alibaba had been quietly working behind the scenes, preparing to challenge them both. The company wasn't just another competitor—it was one of the largest tech conglomerates in the world, armed with the resources, infrastructure, and deep integration into China's digital ecosystem to push AI to a new level. And it made its intentions clear with the announcement of Qwen 2.5—a model Alibaba claimed could outperform not just DeepSeek's R1, but even OpenAI's GPT-4.

The announcement was calculated, strategic, and perfectly timed. Unlike DeepSeek, which had emerged from relative obscurity, Alibaba was an established behemoth, known for its dominance in cloud computing, e-commerce, and AI-driven enterprise solutions. The company wasn't merely trying to prove that it could build a competitive AI model—it was signaling that it was ready to take the lead in the AI arms race, both in China and globally.

The world's attention turned to the benchmarks. Alibaba released performance comparisons showing Qwen 2.5 excelling in key areas where AI models were traditionally judged: reasoning, mathematical problem-solving, coding proficiency, and linguistic versatility. In particular, it claimed superior results in Chinese-language comprehension, an area where even OpenAI's models had struggled. This alone gave Alibaba a major strategic advantage—it meant Qwen 2.5 could dominate AI adoption within China, where billions of dollars were flowing into AI-powered automation, enterprise solutions, and government-backed initiatives.

But the real question wasn't just about its performance in controlled tests. The real measure of an AI model's power came from real-world applications. Could Qwen 2.5 truly outthink, outwrite, and outreason GPT-4 in unpredictable scenarios? Could it surpass DeepSeek's R1, which had already stunned the industry with its efficiency?

Skepticism followed Alibaba's announcement almost immediately. OpenAI had set the bar impossibly high with its GPT-4 models, which were trained on vast computational resources backed by Microsoft's deep pockets. DeepSeek, on the other hand, had sparked intense speculation about whether its rapid success was the result of stolen intelligence rather than pure innovation. Now, Alibaba was claiming to leapfrog both—but where was the independent verification?

Some analysts believed that Alibaba's AI strategy wasn't purely about benchmark performance. Instead, it was about scale and deployment. Unlike OpenAI, which was still figuring out how to make AI profitable at an enterprise level, Alibaba already controlled one of the world's largest cloud computing platforms—Alibaba Cloud. This meant that Qwen 2.5 could be deployed across Alibaba's vast ecosystem, integrating seamlessly into businesses, government projects, and consumer services across China.

If Alibaba's claims about Qwen 2.5 held up, it would mark a significant shift in the AI power balance. OpenAI had the advantage of first-mover status and cutting-edge research. DeepSeek had stunned the world with its ultra-efficient training methods. But Alibaba had something neither of them did—control over one of the largest digital infrastructures on the planet.

The race wasn't just about who could build the best AI anymore. It was about who could deploy it at scale, integrate it into global industries, and make it indispensable. And with Qwen 2.5, Alibaba wasn't just looking to compete—it was looking to dominate.

Alibaba's entry into the AI arms race wasn't just about launching a powerful model—it was about leveraging an entire ecosystem that could integrate AI into nearly every aspect of digital infrastructure. Unlike OpenAI, which primarily functioned as a research-driven AI company reliant on Microsoft for cloud computing power, Alibaba already had one of the most extensive and self-sufficient AI ecosystems in the world.

At the heart of this advantage was Alibaba Cloud, a division that had grown into China's largest cloud computing provider and one of the top three globally, competing directly with Amazon Web Services and Microsoft Azure. This wasn't just about storage and computing power—Alibaba Cloud powered businesses, government operations, financial services, and even China's e-commerce backbone. The same infrastructure that handled billions of transactions on Taobao, Tmall, and Alipay could now be used to train, deploy, and optimize AI models like Qwen 2.5 at an unprecedented scale.

This meant that Alibaba's approach to AI was fundamentally different from that of OpenAI or DeepSeek. While OpenAI was focused on advancing the intelligence of its models and licensing them to businesses, and DeepSeek was trying to prove it could match OpenAI's capabilities despite limited resources, Alibaba was playing a much bigger game. It was integrating AI into everything—enterprise solutions, logistics, finance, cloud services, smart cities, and even government projects.

Unlike DeepSeek, which still had to rely on external cloud infrastructure, Alibaba had full control over its AI operations. This autonomy allowed it to optimize hardware usage, scale AI models at a lower cost, and embed AI deeply into its business empire. Whether it was AI-powered fraud detection for Alipay, automated supply chain optimization for Alibaba's logistics network, or hyper-personalized recommendations on its e-commerce platforms,

Qwen 2.5 wasn't just a chatbot—it was a strategic tool that could enhance Alibaba's trillion-dollar empire.

But the company's AI ambitions didn't stop at China. Alibaba had been expanding its cloud services internationally, with data centers across Asia, Europe, and the Middle East. If Qwen 2.5 proved to be as powerful as Alibaba claimed, it wouldn't just be competing with OpenAI in terms of intelligence—it would be competing in infrastructure, global deployment, and enterprise AI solutions.

This approach put Alibaba in a category of its own. While OpenAI was pushing the boundaries of AGI research and DeepSeek was drawing attention for its unexpected breakthroughs, Alibaba was ensuring that AI became an everyday, embedded technology—one that businesses, governments, and entire industries would rely on.

And that raised a new question: If Alibaba could integrate Qwen 2.5 into every layer of China's digital infrastructure, was there any limit to how much control it could exert over the future of AI?

Alibaba's decision to announce Qwen 2.5 during Lunar New Year was anything but random. It was a calculated strategic move designed to capture the largest possible audience at the perfect moment—not just in China, but across the global financial and technology sectors.

Lunar New Year is the biggest holiday in China, a time when people step back from their daily routines, spend more time online, and pay closer attention to major news. The timing ensured that Alibaba's AI dominance would be the center of discussion across Chinese media, business networks, and government circles. More importantly, it allowed Alibaba to control the narrative, positioning itself as China's AI leader just as DeepSeek was beginning to gain global attention.

But the effects of Alibaba's announcement reached far beyond China. The global AI industry had already been shaken by DeepSeek's rise, with investors scrambling to understand how a relatively unknown Chinese startup had managed to challenge OpenAI. Now, with Alibaba—an established tech giant—stepping in with an even stronger claim, the financial markets reacted in real time.

The biggest impact was felt by Nvidia. The company's stock, which had been riding high on the AI boom, plummeted by $600 billion in market value in a single day, marking the worst single-day loss in U.S. stock market history. Nvidia had long been viewed as the key enabler of AI progress, supplying the world's most powerful GPUs to OpenAI, Google, Microsoft, and nearly every AI company operating at scale. But if China's AI firms were proving they could build competitive models using fewer Nvidia chips—or worse, domestic alternatives like Huawei's Ascend 910C—the long-term demand for Nvidia's technology suddenly seemed uncertain.

For investors, the panic was driven by a fundamental shift in the AI landscape. If companies like DeepSeek could train an OpenAI-level model using just 2,000 GPUs instead of 25,000, it meant that the AI hardware market wasn't as dependent on sheer computational power as once believed. And if Alibaba's Qwen 2.5 could dominate China's enterprise and cloud AI market, it meant that Nvidia's best customers—Chinese firms—might soon be relying on homegrown alternatives instead.

The ripple effect extended to other AI-driven companies. OpenAI and Microsoft saw a dip in investor confidence, as the prospect of real competition from China raised concerns about whether they could maintain their dominant position. Meanwhile, Chinese tech stocks surged, with investors betting that Alibaba, Baidu, and other AI-heavy firms would emerge as global leaders.

But the biggest concern for U.S. investors wasn't just competition—it was control. If China had found a way to push forward in AI despite Washington's restrictions on Nvidia chips, then the entire strategy of using hardware limitations to slow China's AI progress was now in doubt. The fear was no longer just about Alibaba or DeepSeek—it was about whether the U.S. had already lost the ability to contain China's AI expansion.

Alibaba had made its move at the perfect moment, turning a routine AI announcement into a declaration of power. And as the markets continued to react, one thing became increasingly clear: The AI arms race was no longer just a competition—it was an all-out economic and technological war.

Chapter 7: The Truth Behind AI Training and Cost Efficiency

The rapid advancements in artificial intelligence have been fueled not just by raw computing power but by AI scaling laws—the underlying principles that dictate how models improve as they grow larger and more sophisticated. The fundamental idea behind scaling laws is that bigger models trained on larger datasets with more computing power will consistently yield better performance. OpenAI, DeepSeek, and Alibaba have all built their AI breakthroughs on these principles, but the key challenge has always been how to optimize AI training while keeping costs manageable.

Traditionally, training state-of-the-art AI models like GPT-4, DeepSeek R1, and Qwen 2.5 required immense computational resources. The more complex a model, the more data it needs, the more GPUs are required, and the longer it takes to fine-tune. OpenAI, for example, relied on over 25,000 Nvidia H100 GPUs to train GPT-4, with a rumored budget exceeding $100 million. In contrast, DeepSeek claimed to have built its model using just 2,000 H800 GPUs for $5.6 million—a claim that shocked the AI world and raised speculation about whether it had used alternative techniques, including extracting knowledge from OpenAI's outputs.

One of the most effective cost-saving strategies that AI companies employ is algorithmic optimization—making models smarter, not just bigger. Techniques like mixture-of-experts (MoE) allow AI models to activate only certain sections of their neural networks at a time, rather than engaging the entire system for every task. This drastically reduces the amount of computing power needed per query, making AI more efficient and scalable for real-world applications.

But beyond the mathematical efficiencies, another crucial technique has emerged as the gold standard for fine-tuning AI models—Reinforcement Learning from Human Feedback (RLHF).

RLHF has become the secret weapon behind the best AI models on the market. Rather than relying purely on pre-trained neural networks, AI systems learn and improve through direct human interaction, allowing them to refine their responses based on real-world preferences, ethical considerations, and contextual understanding. This technique played a crucial role in shaping OpenAI's ChatGPT, making it more accurate, engaging, and aligned with human expectations than earlier AI models.

DeepSeek and Alibaba both adopted RLHF in their AI training, aiming to replicate OpenAI's success in making AI models feel more human-like in conversation, reasoning, and decision-making. Reinforcement learning allows AI systems to prioritize better responses over time, filtering out undesirable outputs and adapting to complex, nuanced human queries.

The widespread use of RLHF also raises critical questions about how AI models develop their "personalities" and decision-making processes. While this technique ensures AI aligns with human preferences, it also introduces biases, as models learn from human annotators who may have their own cultural or political perspectives. The more AI models rely on human feedback loops, the more subjective and potentially manipulated their responses become—a major concern as companies like OpenAI, DeepSeek, and Alibaba compete for dominance in shaping AI's role in society.

With scaling laws and RLHF as their guiding frameworks, AI companies are no longer just competing on raw computational power—they are competing on efficiency, adaptability, and the ability to create AI that truly understands human intent. This shift is what allows companies like DeepSeek to claim it trained a world-class AI at a fraction of the cost, and Alibaba to integrate AI seamlessly into its vast digital empire.

But as these optimizations continue, one key question remains: Will there ever be a limit to how far AI can scale? And if not, what happens when artificial intelligence surpasses even human-level reasoning? The answer to that question may shape the next phase of the AI arms race.

DeepSeek's sudden rise to AI prominence was met with both awe and skepticism. The company's claim that it had trained a GPT-4-level model using just 2,000 Nvidia H800 GPUs and a budget of $5.6 million defied industry norms. OpenAI, backed by Microsoft's billions, had required over 25,000 H100 GPUs and an estimated $100 million to train its flagship model. If DeepSeek's numbers were accurate, it had either developed a revolutionary new training method that slashed costs—or it had found an alternative way to reach the same results.

At the heart of the debate was efficiency. AI models traditionally require enormous amounts of computational power because they undergo an exhaustive training process, learning from vast datasets, optimizing billions of parameters, and running countless iterations to improve accuracy.

The industry had long accepted that more data, more GPUs, and more money resulted in better AI. DeepSeek, however, appeared to break this rule, suggesting that it had found a way to train smarter, not harder.

One possibility was that DeepSeek had implemented aggressive optimization techniques to maximize efficiency. Leading AI labs, including OpenAI, have been experimenting with methods such as mixture-of-experts (MoE), which allows AI models to selectively activate only certain portions of their neural networks at a time, rather than engaging the full model for every query. This approach significantly reduces computational overhead, allowing companies to train and run AI models at lower costs. If DeepSeek had developed an advanced version of MoE or another breakthrough training method, it could have explained how it achieved high-level performance on limited hardware.

Another possibility was that DeepSeek had found ways to bypass the most computationally expensive phases of training. Reinforcement Learning from Human Feedback (RLHF), the technique used by OpenAI to refine ChatGPT, is notoriously resource-intensive because it requires large-scale human evaluation and multiple rounds of retraining. If DeepSeek had developed a more automated or streamlined version of RLHF, it could have avoided one of the biggest cost drivers in AI training.

Yet, despite these potential optimizations, many in the AI industry remained skeptical. The efficiency gap between DeepSeek and OpenAI was simply too wide for conventional improvements alone to explain. If DeepSeek had achieved such a massive leap in cost-effectiveness, why hadn't OpenAI, Google, or Meta—companies with access to the world's best AI researchers—already done the same?

This led to a more controversial theory: Had DeepSeek taken a shortcut by leveraging OpenAI's intelligence?

If DeepSeek had used AI distillation—training its model based on GPT-4's outputs rather than starting from scratch—it would have dramatically reduced the amount of computing power needed. By systematically querying OpenAI's API and analyzing its responses, DeepSeek could have reverse-engineered OpenAI's intelligence, skipping the most expensive steps in AI training.

This theory aligned with Microsoft's reported findings of suspicious activity linked to DeepSeek within OpenAI's API. If DeepSeek had extracted large volumes of OpenAI-generated data and fine-tuned its model on those outputs, it would explain how it was able to achieve comparable performance at a fraction of the cost.

The efficiency question remained unresolved. If DeepSeek had genuinely developed a smarter, more cost-effective training method, it would mark one of the biggest breakthroughs in AI development—one that could reshape the economics of artificial intelligence and challenge the assumption that only billion-dollar companies could create cutting-edge models.

But if the real secret to DeepSeek's efficiency wasn't innovation, but rather a well-executed act of AI knowledge extraction, then the implications were far more disruptive. It would mean that any AI company could potentially replicate OpenAI's intelligence without ever building a massive training infrastructure—turning proprietary AI research into something that could be systematically absorbed and redeployed by competitors.

As OpenAI and Microsoft intensified their investigation, the truth behind DeepSeek's efficiency advantage remained one of the biggest unanswered questions in AI. If DeepSeek had truly discovered a radically cheaper way to train AI, the entire industry would have to rethink how AI development was done. But if it had simply found a loophole to shortcut OpenAI's progress, then the AI race wasn't just about innovation anymore—it was about who could protect their knowledge from being extracted and repurposed by competitors.

The rise of DeepSeek and Alibaba in the AI race wasn't just about raw computational power or access to specialized hardware—it reignited a bigger debate about the role of open-source research in AI breakthroughs. For years, artificial intelligence had thrived on collaboration and publicly shared advancements, with researchers across institutions publishing their findings openly to accelerate progress. But as AI became a trillion-dollar industry and a new frontier for geopolitical competition, companies that had once championed openness—like OpenAI—were now fiercely protecting their proprietary models.

The question now was whether DeepSeek and Alibaba had truly out-innovated U.S. AI firms—or whether they had simply leveraged the massive amount of freely available research to catch up.

In the early days of deep learning, much of the foundational work behind large language models was built on academic research, shared code, and collaborative studies. OpenAI itself had published key papers detailing breakthroughs in transformer architectures, model scaling, and Reinforcement Learning from Human Feedback (RLHF), all of which laid the groundwork for today's AI advancements. Meta's LLaMA models were another example—highly capable AI systems made open-source, allowing anyone to build upon them.

China's AI firms had been particularly effective at studying, modifying, and optimizing publicly available AI research. Unlike companies in the U.S., which often competed for proprietary dominance, Chinese firms operated within an ecosystem that encouraged rapid iteration based on external findings. This gave companies like DeepSeek and Alibaba a strategic advantage—they could skip past years of trial-and-error research by directly implementing techniques that had already been proven by U.S. companies.

DeepSeek's rise was a case study in how open research could be leveraged for competitive advantage. If DeepSeek had built its AI on top of publicly available models and fine-tuned them with proprietary optimizations, it wouldn't technically be theft—it would be strategic adaptation. The real controversy, however, stemmed from accusations that DeepSeek had not just used open research, but had actively extracted knowledge from OpenAI's closed-source API, giving it an unfair shortcut to intelligence replication.

Alibaba's approach was less controversial but equally effective. With Qwen 2.5, Alibaba had positioned itself as China's leading AI powerhouse, but it had done so by operating within a system where AI development was less about pure innovation and more about mass deployment and integration into enterprise services. Unlike OpenAI, which aimed for breakthroughs in artificial general intelligence (AGI), Alibaba's strategy was to scale AI across cloud computing, finance, logistics, and e-commerce, creating real-world applications faster than U.S. firms.

The divide between open-source AI and proprietary AI was now a defining issue in the global AI race. On one hand, open research had been the fuel that allowed AI to reach its current state, and restricting access to knowledge could slow innovation across the board. On the other hand, companies like OpenAI and Microsoft now faced a harsh reality—if they continued to publish their advancements, competitors (especially from China) could use that knowledge to close the gap without having to invest nearly as much.

This shift had already begun to change the industry. OpenAI, which had once positioned itself as an open research lab, had increasingly restricted access to its findings, opting to release AI models as paid products rather than share their architectures.

Google and Microsoft were following a similar path, limiting how much of their AI advancements were made available for public study.

But with China's AI sector thriving on adaptation, the question remained: Could the U.S. afford to keep AI breakthroughs locked away, or would restricting access only encourage competitors to develop alternative pathways to the same goal?

At the heart of this debate was a fundamental reality: The AI arms race was no longer just about who had the best models—it was about who had the smartest strategy. DeepSeek and Alibaba had proven that AI innovation wasn't just about research—it was about execution, efficiency, and leveraging every available advantage.

And if OpenAI and its U.S. counterparts weren't careful, they could find themselves outpaced not because of a lack of innovation, but because they had given their competitors a roadmap to follow.

Chapter 8: The Real-World Impact of the AI Arms Race

The rise of advanced AI models like OpenAI's GPT-4, DeepSeek's R1, and Alibaba's Qwen 2.5 isn't just a battle for technological supremacy—it's a fundamental shift in how work, productivity, and economic systems function. The impact of these breakthroughs on global job markets is already undeniable, as AI's ability to perform complex tasks more efficiently than humans reshapes entire industries.

For years, automation has been creeping into various sectors, from manufacturing and logistics to customer service and data analysis. But the latest wave of AI, powered by massive language models and reinforcement learning, is extending automation beyond routine, repetitive work and into areas once considered uniquely human—creative writing, software development, legal analysis, financial planning, and even scientific research.

The implications for employment are staggering. Many entry-level and mid-tier jobs that rely on knowledge work—such as content creation, programming, marketing, and even legal assistance—are being automated at a speed that few anticipated. Companies no longer need large teams of junior analysts, writers, or coders when an AI model can generate reports, draft contracts, debug code, and even handle customer inquiries in multiple languages, all within seconds.

At the same time, AI isn't just replacing jobs—it's also creating new ones. Companies are now hiring AI trainers, prompt engineers, and model auditors to refine these systems. The demand for AI ethicists, cybersecurity specialists, and machine learning engineers is growing rapidly, as businesses seek to integrate AI into their operations responsibly. But the challenge is clear: The jobs being displaced by AI aren't necessarily the same as the ones being created.

For workers in traditional roles, the transition to an AI-driven economy is fraught with uncertainty. Will AI be a tool that enhances human productivity, or will it become a replacement for human labor at an unprecedented scale? The answer depends largely on how companies like OpenAI, DeepSeek, and Alibaba choose to deploy their technologies.

One of the biggest questions in the AI revolution is accessibility. If AI remains an exclusive tool controlled by a few major corporations, it could lead to further economic inequality, where only the wealthiest firms and individuals benefit from AI-driven productivity gains. However, if companies make AI more affordable and widely available, it could usher in a new era where small businesses, entrepreneurs, and individuals have access to the same powerful tools as billion-dollar enterprises.

OpenAI has taken a hybrid approach, offering free access to ChatGPT with premium subscription tiers for more powerful versions. DeepSeek, on the other hand, launched with completely free access to its AI assistant, which contributed to its rapid rise in popularity. Alibaba, with its dominance in cloud computing and enterprise AI, is uniquely positioned to integrate AI into its vast ecosystem of businesses and government services, potentially making AI a ubiquitous part of daily life in China.

The competition between these companies is about more than just who builds the smartest AI—it's about who controls access to intelligence itself. If OpenAI, DeepSeek, and Alibaba all move toward making AI cheaper and more widely available, it could accelerate global innovation at an unprecedented scale. But if they limit access to those who can afford high-tier AI services, then AI could become a tool of the elite, further widening the digital divide.

Regardless of how accessibility unfolds, one thing is certain: The AI-driven transformation of the job market is already underway. Some will adapt, learning how to work alongside AI to increase their efficiency and capabilities. Others may find themselves pushed out of industries that no longer require as much human labor. The only real question left is whether society will be ready for the scale of disruption that's coming—or if the AI revolution will reshape the global workforce before anyone has a chance to prepare.

As AI advances at an unprecedented pace, security concerns are becoming one of the most pressing issues in the industry. The same breakthroughs that allow AI models to generate human-like responses, solve complex problems, and automate business processes also open the door to espionage, intellectual property theft, and global cybersecurity threats. The rise of DeepSeek and Alibaba's AI dominance has only intensified these fears, forcing companies and governments to rethink how they protect AI models, training data, and proprietary research.

One of the biggest vulnerabilities in AI security is intellectual property theft. AI models are trained on massive datasets, fine-tuned with billions of parameters, and require enormous computational resources—but their outputs can be systematically extracted, replicated, and repurposed. Microsoft's investigation into DeepSeek's activities raised alarms about the possibility that OpenAI's intelligence had been siphoned and distilled into a rival AI model. If this kind of data extraction went unchecked, it could mean that no AI breakthrough is ever truly safe from being reverse-engineered by competitors.

But the risks go far beyond corporate rivalries. AI espionage has now become a matter of national security. Governments are increasingly concerned about how AI could be used in cyber warfare, misinformation campaigns, and automated hacking operations. The ability of AI to generate deepfake content, mimic human behavior in social engineering attacks, and analyze massive amounts of data in real-time makes it a powerful tool for both state-sponsored intelligence agencies and cybercriminal organizations.

In response to these threats, Big Tech has begun fortifying its AI models against potential breaches. Microsoft, Google, Meta, and Amazon—each deeply invested in AI—have all adopted stricter security protocols, closed-source AI models, and limited public access to their most advanced systems. OpenAI, which originally positioned itself as an open research lab, has shifted toward a more secretive and commercialized approach, restricting access to its latest breakthroughs to prevent unauthorized use.

Microsoft, as OpenAI's closest partner and financial backer, has taken the most aggressive stance on AI security. The company's direct involvement in monitoring OpenAI's API for suspicious activity suggests that it views AI knowledge extraction as a real and immediate threat. Google, on the other hand, has adopted a dual strategy—continuing to release open-source AI models like Gemini but limiting the scope of its most powerful versions to prevent misuse.

Meta has chosen to lean into open-source AI, making its LLaMA models freely available to developers, believing that transparency and broad access can outcompete closed systems in the long run. But this approach also raises the risk that foreign entities, including potential adversaries, could study and exploit these models to build their own AI faster than if they had to develop them independently.

Amazon, with its massive AWS cloud computing infrastructure, has positioned itself as a neutral AI provider, offering businesses the ability to build and host their own AI models while keeping a lower profile in the AI arms race. But as competition intensifies, even Amazon may be forced to take a stronger stance on AI security and proprietary protection.

The battle over AI is no longer just about who can build the smartest models—it's about who can protect their intelligence from being stolen, weaponized, or used against them. The ability to safeguard AI systems will determine which companies and nations maintain their technological advantage in the years ahead.

And if the rise of DeepSeek has proven anything, it's that no AI breakthrough is guaranteed to remain exclusive for long. The question now is whether Big Tech can adapt fast enough to secure their AI dominance—or if the next major AI disruption will come from an unexpected player, leveraging knowledge that was never meant to be shared.

As AI advances at a pace that even its own creators struggle to control, governments around the world are realizing that they can no longer afford to be passive observers. The rise of models like GPT-4, DeepSeek R1, and Qwen 2.5 has made one thing clear: AI is no longer just a tool for innovation—it is a strategic asset, an economic powerhouse, and a potential security risk all at once. With that realization comes an inevitable shift: AI regulations are coming, and they will reshape the industry.

The question is no longer if governments will intervene in AI competition—it's how.

The U.S. and China, the two dominant players in the AI arms race, are already taking drastically different approaches. In Washington, policymakers have begun treating AI development as a national security priority, imposing strict export bans on Nvidia's most powerful GPUs to prevent China from accelerating its AI capabilities. These restrictions are aimed at slowing down China's access to cutting-edge hardware, but as DeepSeek and Alibaba have shown, China is quickly adapting, finding alternative ways to train and deploy competitive models.

Meanwhile, China's own AI regulations are not designed to restrict development—instead, they focus on tight government oversight and censorship controls to ensure that AI remains aligned with state objectives. Chinese tech giants like Alibaba, Baidu, and Tencent are required to comply with government directives, meaning that AI development in China is not just driven by corporate competition but also by national strategic interests.

The European Union, often the first to impose tech regulations, has already introduced the AI Act, one of the world's most ambitious attempts to regulate artificial intelligence. The act classifies AI systems based on risk levels, imposing strict compliance requirements on high-risk applications like facial recognition, biometric surveillance, and autonomous decision-making in critical industries. But the EU's approach is largely focused on ethics and consumer protection, whereas the U.S. and China view AI through the lens of global power and security.

In the private sector, companies like Microsoft, Google, and OpenAI are actively lobbying governments to create AI regulations that align with their own business interests. OpenAI's CEO, Sam Altman, has repeatedly called for international AI oversight, suggesting that a global regulatory body could be created to ensure AI remains safe and aligned with human values. But critics argue that such calls for regulation are not entirely altruistic—instead, they could serve to lock in OpenAI's dominance by making it harder for new competitors to emerge.

The most difficult challenge in AI regulation is balancing innovation with security. If governments impose heavy restrictions on AI research and deployment, it could slow progress and prevent smaller players from competing. On the other hand, if AI remains largely unregulated, there is a growing risk that bad actors—whether companies, rogue states, or cybercriminals—could exploit AI for fraud, surveillance, or even autonomous warfare.

There is also the issue of data privacy and bias. AI models are trained on massive datasets, often scraped from the internet, raising legal questions about who owns the data that AI learns from. If companies like OpenAI and Alibaba continue to build AI on publicly available content, should authors, journalists, and artists be compensated? If AI models develop biases that reinforce harmful stereotypes, who is responsible—the company that built the model or the users who deploy it?

Some governments are already preparing to take drastic action. In the U.S., lawmakers are exploring legislation that could restrict AI-generated political content, require disclosure when AI is used in decision-making, and hold AI companies liable for misinformation and biases. In China, AI-generated content is already heavily censored, ensuring that models like Qwen 2.5 remain aligned with government-approved narratives.

The next few years will determine how AI is governed on a global scale. Will countries agree on international AI standards, much like they have for nuclear weapons and climate change policies? Or will AI become a new battleground for geopolitical power struggles, with each nation enforcing its own rules to maintain an advantage?

What is certain is that AI is no longer just an industry—it's a force that will shape economies, societies, and global power structures. The question now is who gets to decide its future.

Conclusion: Who Will Dominate the Future of AI?

The race for AI dominance is far from over. What began as a competition between a handful of research labs has transformed into a global struggle for technological supremacy, with OpenAI, DeepSeek, and Alibaba at the center of an industry that will define the next century. Artificial intelligence is no longer just about who builds the smartest chatbot or the most efficient language model—it is about who controls the future of intelligence itself.

As OpenAI and Microsoft continue their investigation into DeepSeek, the question remains: Was DeepSeek's AI model built through legitimate research, or did it gain an unfair advantage by siphoning OpenAI's knowledge? If OpenAI and Microsoft find concrete evidence of intellectual property theft, it could lead to a high-stakes legal battle, setting a precedent for how AI knowledge is protected in an era where models can be reverse-engineered and distilled at an alarming pace. But if DeepSeek's success was a result of genuine innovation, it could force OpenAI and Microsoft to rethink their strategy, proving that billion-dollar budgets are not the only path to building world-class AI.

Beyond DeepSeek, the AI arms race is shaping up to be a three-way battle between OpenAI and its Western allies, China's tech giants, and new challengers emerging from unexpected corners of the world. OpenAI, with Microsoft's backing, has a head start, but Alibaba's deep integration into China's cloud computing and enterprise sectors gives it a massive strategic advantage. Meanwhile, DeepSeek's mysterious efficiency and disruptive potential make it a wildcard that neither OpenAI nor Alibaba can afford to ignore.

But the battle for AI dominance isn't just about corporate rivalries—it's about how AI will reshape economies, security, and the balance of global power. Governments are now actively intervening in AI competition, recognizing that whoever leads in artificial intelligence will control the digital infrastructure of the future. The U.S. is tightening restrictions on AI chip exports, China is heavily investing in domestic alternatives, and the European Union is laying the groundwork for regulatory oversight that could influence global AI policies.

There are still many unanswered questions. Can DeepSeek provide transparent proof that its AI was developed without leveraging OpenAI's outputs? Will Alibaba's Qwen 2.5 cement its place as the AI leader in China and beyond, challenging OpenAI at a global scale? How will the ongoing rivalry between the U.S. and China shape AI development, and will either side gain a decisive edge, or will innovation become fragmented across geopolitical lines?

One thing is certain: The AI revolution is here. It is no longer a concept of the future—it is unfolding in real-time, disrupting industries, redefining economies, and challenging the very nature of intelligence. Whether AI remains a tool for progress or a weapon for control will depend on the decisions made by governments, corporations, and the engineers who build these systems.

The next phase of AI won't just be about who can build the most powerful models—it will be about who has the vision, the strategy, and the foresight to shape the future. And in this race, no one can afford to fall behind.